T0157372

SACRED VERSES

PART FOUR and EPILOGUE (JOURNEY'S END and SANCTUARY)

GENE JACKSON

iUniverse, Inc.
Bloomington

SACRED VERSES, PART FOUR and EPILOGUE
JOURNEY'S END and SANCTUARY

iUniverse books may be ordered through booksellers or by contacting:

*iUniverse
1663 Liberty Drive
Bloomington, IN 47403
www.iuniverse.com
1-800-Authors (1-800-288-4677)*

*ISBN: 978-1-4759-3502-8 (sc)
ISBN: 978-1-4759-3501-1 (e)*

Printed in the United States of America

iUniverse rev. date: 07/03/2012

To Chris:

". . .for he was like, had he been tried,

to have proved most royal."

and, To David,

the Spartan.

"Only to gods in heaven
    Comes no old age or death of anything;
        All else is turmoiled by our master, Time.
        Earth's glory fades,
           And mankind's strength will go away;
Faith dies, and Unfaith blossoms like a flower.
    And who can find, in the open streets of men
        Or secret places of his own heart's love
          One wind blow true forever?"

Sophocles
"Oedipus at Colonnae"

"But soon we too shall die,
    And all memory of those we loved will have left the earth,
        And we ourselves shall be loved for a while and then forgotten.
But the love will have been enough;
    All those impulses of love return to the love that made them.
Even memory is not necessary for love;

There is a land of the living and a land of the dead,
    And the bridge is love,
        The only survival,
           The only meaning."

T. Wilder
"The Bridge of San Luis Rey"

AUTHOR'S NOTE

The *Divine Comedy* of Dante Alighieri was written in a strict rhyme scheme of *Terza Rima*. This is feasible in Italian but not in English, and therefore all of these verses are in sonnet form. By far, the majority are Italian (or Petrarchian), but each chapter ends in one or more Shakespearean sonnets. This is, as far as I am aware, the longest sonnet sequence in English literature. The verses are described as *Sacred*, not in the sense of *Holy* or *Devout* but in the classical or medieval sense of relating to the spiritual or intellectual universe, instead of the body and physical world, which would be *Profane*.

In the first volume, a young man (who has suffered a great loss in his life), has sought an overview of the physical universe in which we live, and this may be considered equivalent to the *Inferno* of Dante. The second volume (during which the young man matures) is concerned with philosophy, an understanding of human mind and thought, and an intellectual attempt to understand the universe. Therefore, it could be regarded as a parallel to the *Purgatorio* of Dante. In the third volume (and in this, the fourth and concluding part) he has aged due to his travels, but still needs to explore the spiritual aspects of our world, and this may be considered as a counterpart to Dante's *Paradisio*.

In each of these endeavors he has had a mentor to guide his journey. In the first volume it was Stephen Hawking (a pre-eminent modern physicist). In the second he was led by Will and Ariel Durant (historians of civilization). For his spiritual quest in parts three and four his mentor is Mother Teresa (a modern saint and source of moral guidance). At the beginning and the end of his journey he encounters Sophocles, one of the great Greek playwrights and philosophers.

At the end of this volume and of his quest, when he has absorbed all of the known features of the universe and of our lives, he is reunited in the epilogue with the loss he originally suffered and is reconciled to the realities of our existence.

VOLUME THREE

JOURNEY'S END and SANCTUARY

REMEMBRANCE

THE JOURNEY TO DATE

Now far past half-way in my journey home
I felt exhausted, yet with much to do,
I knew I must go on, and look into
The universe of values; I would roam
Through twisting passageways, a catacomb
Which someday might become an open view
Of sunlight, sky and stars, a retinue
Replacing weightless light, a monochrome.
For this is what my prior life had been:
When I began, my world was colorless,
Not even black and white, but gray-on-gray,
I could remember many seasons when
My life went on serenely, without stress
And vast emotion seemed so far away.

But then one winter night, as has been told,
The entire world of which I was aware
Dissolved into chaotic loss, a bare
And naked landscape that I watched unfold.
There was no *new* to take the place of *old*,
Nor *color* to be pictured, anywhere,
But only neutral shadows in the air,
The only sound a distant bell that tolled.
But then I met a man upon a beach
Who knew the same emotions that I felt,
The loneliness and sense of isolation;
And from this understanding he could teach
Realities that each of us are dealt
And ways to re-establish our foundation.

He showed the path that I must follow now
To reach awareness of the universe,
The long and winding way I must traverse
To find those secrets fortune will allow;
And hopefully I would discover how
These facets of my life, complex, diverse,
Would fit together, possibly reverse
The loss that I had undergone somehow.
He indicated that there were three ways
That taken all together formed a whole,
The sum of all the world and of our lives.
The first of these was *physical*, a phase
Of life and of the universe, its goal
Was balance, without which no one survives.

The second phase was *intellectual*,
The rational response to life that men
Bring forth to serve as explanation when
The universe seems unconventional.
The world misunderstood is mystical,
And therefore will require a regimen
Of serious analysis, and then
Perhaps it will be understandable.
But when the universe is threatening,
And reason cannot serve as reassurance,
Then *transcendental faith* will be the test
Of whether one survives bewildering,
Chaotic tragic life, and with endurance
Completes the play in which he is a guest.

And so it was, throughout the centuries
(That man has wondered who, in truth he is,
What roles within the drama will be his,
And how he will enact each one of these),
That many priests and prophets had arisen,
Each with unique (and clashing) explanations
To clarify, define these situations,
And liberate the people from their prison;
For that is how our lives may often seem
When limited by lack of understanding.
It has been said: "The unexamined life
Is not worth living;" it may be a dream,
A flight into the air without a landing,
Or chaos, disarray, internal strife.

And this is why I made my journey through
The realm of physics and its demonstration
Of all the circumstances since creation
That each of us has known, or thought we knew,
Beginning with the Greeks, who overthrew
The ancient mystic forms of revelation
In favor of more rational causation;
Precise analysis was judged as true.
Much later (by a span of centuries),
Appeared the greatest of astronomers,
And then unequalled minds to synthesize
This knowledge with their own analyses.
Their reasoned verdict was that what occurs
Is as it is, could not be otherwise.

The ultimate in modern abstract thought
Reverberates between the relativity
Of Einstein and the ones who disagree,
Who feel a comprehensive scheme which ought
To clarify the universe is caught
More clearly by the quantum theory;
And thus the cosmic singularity
Is fractured, its equations come to naught.
And yet, the ones who scan our universe
(The physical, substantial side of it),
Have never ceased to seek a unified
Link between the forces that disperse
The stars and those that do the opposite;
Their failure leaves us all unsatisfied.

Because of this frustration early-on,
Philosophers began to give significance
To theories of thought, whose relevance
To life's realities were finely drawn.
But hardly was one exposition gone
Than others would arise (and not by chance),
They jousted back and forth for dominance,
But none of them became a paragon.
The *realist* described the world that *is*,
Idealists the one they *wish* it were;
Thus Plato concentrated on *perfections*
While Aristotle answered this with his
Conception of *reality*, a blur
Of knowledge reaching out in all directions.

This double thread of thought has been entwined
In various disguises over time,
And cloned itself (like dance in pantomime)
Into philosophies, aware or blind.
Theology (St. Augustine combined
With Thomas, St. Aquinas, as the prime
Example) reached the ultimate sublime
Precursor on which modern thought aligned.
For Augustine led on to Thomas Moore,
And then in turn Baruch (or Benedict)
Spinoza, then Voltaire, Jean-Jacques Rousseau
And modern thinkers who would underscore
(Like Kant and his *imperatives*) the strict
Divorce between *ideals* and *status quo*.

But Aristotle (through Aquinas) found
His legacy throughout the centuries
By means of rational analyses
Of many thinkers (some of which were sound).
Among these Machiavelli, with profound
Distrust of faultless perfect qualities,
Who saw things as they are, not fantasies,
But stark reality, or its rebound.
Assessing Borgias, or the Medici
He found that each contained a mortal flaw,
And postulated that we all did, too.
Behavior (read: "Self interest"), was free
Of any abstract principles or law
And we are free to act just as we do.

This line of thought perverted Aristotle,
But running on to Bacon, Hobbes, Descartes
(And David Hume who was their counterpart),
Denied ideals of Plato as pure twaddle.
And then the Existentialists (full throttle)
Proclaimed the suffering of man, whose heart,
Created to be broken from the start,
Was like *ideals*, a Genie in a bottle.
In current thinking and philosophy
Which recognizes: "Life is not idyllic,
And yet it does have meaning", we must seek
To re-establish our *humanity*
Which is, through Dietrich Bonhoeffer, Paul Tillich,
And Martin Buber's *Ich und du*, unique.

But understanding, too, was not enough;
I found in spite of knowledge of the world,
And of the planets and the stars that whirled
Around and past each other, and the puff
That formed our universe, and followed rough
Approximate essential laws that curled
Around each other, all of what was hurled
Out into space came back as altered stuff.
Yet all around was still a mystery,
Despite the physicists, astronomers,
And all who write equations on the wall;
But just as cryptic is the unity
Attempted by profuse philosophers
Whose cleverness is like a waterfall.

A waterfall or similar cascade
Delivers water, with its energy
From heights above, and somewhat carelessly,
Depending on its channels (that were made
By other forces in the past), its grade,
And course and flow that all of us can see,
But never alters its activity;
So caught within its flow, we are afraid.
And this is why *religions* took their place
Beside the other disciplines, to solve
Conundrums and enigmas that remain
Despite the long unraveling of space
And explanations of how stars revolve,
Which abstract thinkers analyzed in vain.

For even science plus philosophy
Was insufficient still to understand
What was an *accident* , and what was *planned*
And why my life was as it was for me.
And so I sought the Master, Lao-Tze
Whose concept of the universe had spanned
A mystic never-ending *way*, a grand
Pathway through our lives, but silently.
And then the *Teacher*, he whose Middle Way
Came half-way in between the *Realists*
And those who thought that *Love* (and *Heaven* too)
Would lead us on and forward, not astray,
(And these I could identify: *Idealists*);
Confucius found the path between the two.

And then the Buddha, he who was awake;
The world, he felt, was in a womb of sleep,
And moral living only that of sheep
Who followed blindly into life's mistake.
He spoke in threads of thought, and would forsake
The pain of life, which causes us to weep,
Brings much distress, and nothing we should keep;
Instead, he showed a pathway we should take.
And then I met an ancient patriarch
Who prophesied of God, his Holy Will,
And those, through centuries, who went astray.
Isaiah's view of life, austere and stark
Maintained we must "Awake, Repent", but still
Held out this hope: we might cast sin away.

The search had taken many years, my youth,
My confidence and innocence as well.
The energy that I once had, in truth
Was not sufficient to prevent the Hell
That I descended into; still, from there
I could look upward to a Universe
Of understanding and of reason, where
My ignorance and blindness would disperse.
And this in turn would lead to open sky,
The realm of Heaven, that which I had sought
Through all this time, and which could clarify
The many lessons which I had been taught.
So after this, a time to think and rest,
I found I must return, and end my quest.

THE SOLDIER AND STOIC

The road ahead was wide and clear and straight,
The work of Roman civil engineers;
It even now could illustrate their fears
Of things irregular, that deviate
From measurements that they could calculate.
The highways led from centers to frontiers,
(Though none were built by willing volunteers,
Because the labor there was far too great).
The soldier, not the tourist, was the reason
The road was surveyed, paved, and excavated
Through forests, elevations and depressions,
So that an army could, in any season
Move quickly to a region designated
Strategic for defense, or for aggressions.

But pilgrims, too, could use the road, as I
Now found it necessary, since the rain
Had come; the constant soaking of the plain
And mud in all directions showed me why
The Romans built their highways firm and high.
The night had come, and gone, and come again,
And on a mission seemingly insane,
I struggled, hoping only to stay dry.
But as I reached the stage of desperation,
(Between the dark, the fog, the frigid air,
The rain, the wind, and clothes far worse than damp),
Ahead there was a vague configuration
Of geometric shapes that formed a square,
And then became a military camp.

The pickets met me at the outer gate,
And very quickly they could verify
That this forsaken tramp was not a spy,
Bedraggled, tired and inarticulate.
Allowing me to enter in this state,
They pointed to a place I could be dry,
But I could tell, and they did not deny,
The army was about to re-locate.
The tents were situated with precision,
Along a grid, as if by measurement,
The single lighted one was in the center.
As I approached, with honest indecision,
The sentry challenged me before the tent,
And indicated then that I might enter.

The soldier in his military tent
Was waiting, seated at a desk, erect,
And writing "To Himself" with circumspect
Attention to his moral argument.
Commanding legions with a diligent
And skillful self-control did not deflect
The meditations of his intellect,
Or change a philosophic temperament.
In six long years, he conquered the Sarmations;
He fought the Lombards, finally subdued
Along the Danube, Iazyges and Chatti,
And many other hostile tribes and nations.
But during these campaigns, he still pursued
Inquiries into life and destiny.

Inside his tent, I met his neutral gaze,
He stood with courtesy, did not salute;
(A general who meets a new recruit
Does not enlist potential protégés).
His eyes looked at me frankly, to appraise
My attitude; could he have absolute
Assurances that I would not dispute
His thoughts, or interfere in other ways?
"I hope you will forgive a soldier, who
Is not accustomed to a free debate.
There is no military arbitration,
For we give orders, and accept them, too;
The soldiers must to officers relate,
The Emperor to God and meditation."

"I have been called a pagan; in defense,
I say: 'In public life I have employed
The rituals of state, myself enjoyed
A far more personal experience.'
I answer those who charge irreverence:
'The value of our lives would be destroyed
By living in a universe devoid
Of any God, or gods, or Providence.'
I cannot tolerate philosophy
Which conjures up a single abstract thought
And argues back and forth with verbal strife
Until arriving at Infinity.
Far better if it learned, and then it taught
A school of virtue, and a way of life."

"A king can be disciple to a slave,
Or money-lender, or an artisan.
Nobility and honor thus can span
A spectrum of the fortunes heaven gave.
For if the true-oppressed can still behave
With dignity, the rich vulgarian
Can see that pleasure is a charlatan,
Restraint a virtue, luxury a knave.
The key to life is always moderation,
For passions lead to excess and disorder,
Lay waste inherent logic of the whole,
Disturb the rational equilibration;
For every impulse has its normal border
And every part must play its modest role."

"They say our way of life is cold, austere,
Denying all the passions and desires;
This is not so, philosophy requires
Commitment that the student persevere
Beyond all limits. It will interfere
With frivolous pursuits, its inner fires
Consume all else; the search for truth requires
Our lives, an all-encompassing career.
The truly cold and sterile school of thought
Is that of Epicurus and Lucretius,
Where earthly pleasures are the only way
To tolerate existence; dearly-bought,
Their price: a view of life that is facetious
A sense of heaven empty and blasé."

"I will admit to you: I do not know
If such a thing as immortality
Exists; if so, there is no guarantee
That I would merit such a state. Although
A man might dream of this scenario,
The gods (or Providence) might disagree.
But live your life with equanimity
And try to reach a virtuous plateau;
For it is possible you may depart
Away from life at any sudden time.
If so, a prudent man would regulate
His every act and impulse of his heart
Toward harmony and peace; this paradigm
Will serve him well, regardless of his fate."

"And he who lives with honor never lies,
But has no rancor for the ones who do;
He keeps his covenants, pays what is due,
Forgiving foolish debts that might arise
From those distressed, but does not patronize
Unfortunates, the poor, or someone who
Has lesser status. He is always true
To any promise, even if unwise.
While he is always generous if rich,
When poor, is still a little generous.
His spirit rises over situations
Where someone is embarrassed, those in which
An awkwardness could be averted; thus
His life is one of constant affirmations."

"For what is judged consistent with the laws
Is just for all, the soldier and barbarian,
The Emperor and common journeyman;
And all must answer to their private flaws.
This structure binds us equally because
The universal state is greater than
A smaller empire, nation, tribe, or clan
And all are citizens, and none withdraws.
This great society must be preserved,
It dominates the individual,
But equally throughout the spectrum; thus,
Rewards and honors may be undeserved,
But harmony and truth are integral
To universal virtue, binding us."

"For perfect knowledge still eludes us all,
And metaphysics is beyond our reach.
The new religion that the Christians preach
Seems full of mystery, irrational.
So what is left to us, the ethical
Who strive to live as Providence would teach?
While facing peril, only this: that each
Prepare with courage, not with ritual.
For danger in your life you cannot see,
For grief and sadness that is not expected,
Keep fortitude and strength in all you do;
As Spartans standing at Thermopylae,
While knowing that the traitor has defected,
And in the end, the Persians will go through."

"A citizen who lives with diligence
Within his life, serene, without excess,
How can he say there is a difference,
A span of fifty years, or more, or less?
The hardship comes to fools who are aspirant
To everlasting life and thus begrudge
Mortality, as though it was a tyrant
Responsible, or some corrupted judge.
But universal Nature sent you here,
And set the framework of your present course.
So live in confidence and not in fear,
And know that at the end this vital source
May not approve, but never will condemn
But celebrate, as with a requiem."

"An actor finishes a one-act play;
Should he complain this earlier conclusion
Deprives him of his rightful chance to say
More lines? But this is merely self-delusion.
For he himself did not create the work;
The one who first had caused its composition,
And then employed him, as one might a clerk,
Controls as well the drama's disposition.
According to your talent, play your role,
Complete the written lines and gestures, then
You must not bargain, wheedle or cajole;
Depart with equanimity, for when
The one who placed you here within this scene
Releases you, he also is serene."

Then he arose, put out the single light;
We went outside, the soldiers struck the tent,
And he reviewed the legions as they went,
All marching onward through the bitter night.
I stood beside him in the rain, despite
The fact there was no need, no precedent;
I still admired his stoic temperament,
Which equaled any monk, or anchorite.
But standing there, I saw him isolated
From all his soldiers, and from me as well,
I wondered whether he had ever known
A love, or was his heart as armor-plated
As was his body, this I could not tell;
So he went on, and I was left alone.

I heard the fading metronomic stamp
Ten thousand boots were making on the road,
And closed my mind upon this episode,
Alone within the great deserted camp.
The rain decreased, but I was still as damp
And cold as I had been; the wind had slowed,
The charcoal of the cooking fires just glowed,
And then I lost the candle in my lamp.
Now with its luminosity withdrawn
I was without my last effective light;
But through the shifting clouds, a single star,
Still brilliant in the growing light of dawn,
Maintaining one true focus in the night,
Observed, unblinking, constant, from afar.

That solitary star, eclipsed by light
That soon would swell, beginning in the east,
Was destined to survive until the night
Again returned, it never truly ceased.
So prophets, kings and soldiers come and go,
And emperors will see their power fade,
And nothing will abide, for all we know,
Except the debts that one day must be paid.
Yet somehow, stars (and virtues) will endure,
Will re-appear when darkness comes once more,
As come it will; if we are insecure,
We must remember how they were before.
And since no one is safe from fate's betrayal,
We need a star, and virtue, to prevail.

The Emperor himself was not immune
To failure, evil fortune and distress;
More isolated than a mere tribune,
He was in danger, due to loneliness.
For consolation, he considered Greek
Philosophy, and God, and Providence,
But found no single concept that could speak
More eloquently than his common sense.
And so he focused on the way to live,
On honor, morals, and on harmony,
The virtues that he felt imperative
To reach a state of equanimity.
His son began the Empire's long decay,
His "Meditations" guide us yet today.

THE SERVANT AT THE GATE

Then in the distance, very near the road,
A mansion stood upon a gentle hill,
A beacon, since above each window-sill
A brilliant square of brightness overflowed
On faces where anticipation showed.
The host of this fantastic domicile
Had not appeared; they waited for him still,
To show their gratitude for what they owed.
The lawn and gardens blue with evening light
Seemed like a scene an artist over- did,
A soft aroma, perfume and cigars,
And people flitting by like moths at night,
Ecstatic with the gaiety, amid
The music, laughter, whispering and stars.

I heard the nightingales in silver cages
Concealed within the trees and out of sight;
They serenaded dusk and fading light
Like vespers have been sung throughout the ages.
The sum of these sensations disengages
A person from reality which might
Intrude upon the scene and disunite
Eternal ecstasy into its stages.
The picture, though, in its entirety,
With sights and sounds and scents so tantalizing
Would certainly entice the traveler
To search for ways to enter easily.
And so it was for me, the dream disguising
The vital, hard-earned traits of character.

There was, enclosing all this grand estate,
(Including all the trimmed and manicured
Surrounding gardens, every inch contoured
And shaped to cleverly accommodate
The pleasure-dome within), a delicate
But strong forbidding fence, that thus ensured
Exclusion, even when it falsely lured
The uninvited to participate.
Each person covets something that he sees
But cannot have (or what another has);
Inside, the grandiose amusement park
With lanterns and with incense hung in trees,
Appeared to be a fairyland, whereas
The world outside seemed comfortless and dark.

There were no walls or towers circled round
But only rigid bars, with spikes on top,
Unwelcoming to strangers who might stop
To look into the marvelous compound.
Well-watered ferns that covered all the ground
Might tempt the dusty traveler to drop
His calloused life upon the road and swap
His hardship for the comfort he had found.
The message of the fence, unpromising,
Was that the passage-way within was steeper
Than any ever could anticipate;
The railings had a single opening,
Whose gate was closed, the solitary keeper
Was firmly standing there to keep the gate.

So, looking for an easy way within,
I walked around the margins of the fence
A full five miles, a half-circumference,
And looked inside at intervals wherein
The forests, ancient as the hills, begin,
And underneath, the early confluence
Of rivulets, which later would condense
Into a river, here the origin.
And through the sequence of the open bars
(Not finding any breach where I could enter),
I saw a place, as holy and enchanted
As any that no strife or chaos mars,
A garden radiating from a center,
That some immortal architect had planted.

The branches of the trees were very high,
Allowing open spaces; light in squares
Descended to the garden where parterres
Made checkered patterns. Shade and sunlight lie
In random patches where a dragonfly
Is seen, not seen, and seen again in pairs
That hover in the dark or lighted airs
Provided by the ever-changing sky.
On study of the smoky, stately scene
The garden seemed to be a grand arcade
With lofty arches, each supporting tree
In columns spaced exactly; in between,
The slanted, hazy, inclined shafts of shade
Enfolded sunny spots of greenery.

Then past the gardens that were planned and tended
The random forest faded to seclusion,
And ferns grew wildly there in great profusion,
Light green and fresh, a carpet which ascended
Along the rising ground, and only ended
Against a stream whose vigorous intrusion
Enhanced the forest's wild pristine illusion;
Some trees were down, across the flow extended.
Where four or five had fallen, parallel,
The water slowed and widened to a pond
Expanding quietly, but then at last
It reached the ultimate that it could swell
And tumbled past the dam, but once beyond,
Moved silently again, now smooth and fast.

The surface of the growing river swelled
As it came down from some far-distant hill
Enlarged by many tributaries, still
All sinuous and serpentine, propelled
By heaviness and power, barely held
Within the limits of the earth until
It reached the fallen trees, began to spill
In multiple cascades, all paralleled.
The fence of fallen trees completely spanned
The slowing river, causing it to veer
Above and over as it struggled out.
The river's bed was gravelly, with sand,
The pebbles made the water cold and clear,
And in the river there were many trout.

The trout were holding steady in the deep
Slow-moving water near the dam of trees,
Retaining their position there with ease.
At intervals a drifting trout would leap
Into the current in a sudden steep
Direction to the surface, and would seize
In one great gulp a floating fly, then (these
Exertions ended), seemed to go to sleep.
His surface image floated on the stream,
His shadow moving with the current there,
As in a well- prefigured diagram.
Then unresisting, he would find the seam
Of flowing water, currents leading where
He tightened once again before the dam.

I saw these things from just outside the fence,
And dreamed of placing artificial flies
So lightly on the surface in disguise,
The trout would never know the difference.
In one transfixing moment of suspense
A trout might sense the lure and would arise
To strike the fly, but never realize
The consequence of his experience.
Then I would feel the double-tapered line,
Its tension as I reeled and let it out,
Elation as one finally prevails;
Then love and satisfaction would combine
Upon release of that exhausted trout,
As I would also free the nightingales.

But those outside the fence were powerless;
The metal bars reached far above one's head,
The sharpened points on top prohibited
Clandestine or unauthorized access.
Not only did outsiders feel distress,
Frustration and a vague but growing dread
Of endless isolation, years ahead,
But just a hint of secret sinfulness.
Else why were some included, some were not?
For some appeared to merit invitations,
And yet they were denied a proper entry.
Were these acquaintances the host forgot?
Did access rest on holy dispensations,
Or on the means with which to bribe the sentry?

Downstream, I saw the river as it ran
On past the fallen trees, serene and clear;
It sank into the ground, to disappear
In secret caves invisible to man,
Its course, thereafter subterranean,
Unseen into the sea. The higher tier
Of brooks and rivulets were not severe
Where bridges crossed them in a single span.
Then dimly through the swift-approaching night
I saw a lantern on each formal bridge,
All colored green and whispering, "You can ….."
They all grew brighter in the fading light,
And so encouraged, I went up the ridge,
But when I reached the top, the rain began.

"The vengeance of the gods", I thought, for there
I found the very limit of the fence,
The most remote of this circumference,
As far as I could be from anywhere
That I might find a refuge, one to share
A roof, a fire, a sheltered residence;
Not even asking any opulence
I needed some relief from my despair.
But this was not to be, for it was dark,
I could not see the trail between the lights;
It was not difficult to go astray.
So once (it was enough) I missed the mark
And stepped on one of many slippery sites,
And down in gross unlovely muck I lay.

I could have been an engineer's pontoon
Laid out across the stream, but even smeared
And muddy I arose and persevered.
On down the farther slope I went, and soon
Was hearing distant laughter and a tune
Designed for carefree dancing; as I neared
The glowing garden all the clouds had cleared
To show a silver wafer of a moon.
The lawn was covered with a canvas net
That kept it dry, but I was not enthused,
For I was very much the worse for wear.
My shoes were squishy and my coat was wet,
My body and my self-respect were bruised,
And I had lost my necktie God knows where.

A hundred lights, each one a cigarette
Were embers in the magic night, ongoing
Like charcoal left to die, and yet still glowing.
Beneath the canvas tent a jazz duet
Was playing, saxophone and clarinet,
And mindless rapture showed no sign of slowing.
Within, champagne and vintage wine were flowing,
And I, outside, was muddy, cold and wet.
To one aware, this episode could teach
That troubles, sure and real, are as they seem;
Experience to me would certify
Tranquility as somewhere out of reach.
Deliverance from grief was still a dream,
And promises of paradise a lie.

Reluctantly, I passed the party by;
The people there were beautiful and dressed
In all the latest fashions, and possessed
One consummate advantage, they were dry.
They noticed no one but themselves, not I
Nor any other person as distressed,
Who by their clothes and manners so unblessed
Would never fit, or hope to qualify.
Their attitude of careless confidence
Was necessary to impress each other,
But had no fundamental introspection;
And all behavior, based upon pretense,
Exclusively absorbed with one another,
Allowed no space for genuine affection.

The life inside the fence was bright and gay,
And everyone seemed happy and amused;
And yet I sensed that one and all abused
Their privilege (for nothing underlay
Their endless celebration), so blasé
They never noticed how it was misused.
So, angry, disappointed and confused,
And sad beyond belief, I turned away.
Disheartened by their lack of reverence
(For evil is morality, perverted),
I went ahead in my disheveled state;
I had but little hope or confidence,
Until I reached the place I thought deserted,
And found the servant standing by the gate.

He looked at me as if he'd always known
That I would come; the middle of the night
Did not distress him, though he always might
Have closed the gate, returned into his own
Small cottage, where he seemed to live alone,
And left the traveler to solve his plight.
Instead, he met me there by candle light,
While standing on the roughened cobblestone.
"I watched you in the afternoon", he said,
"And in the evening and for half the night.
You went around the whole perimeter
While looking for contentment, but instead
You saw a brilliant, superficial sight
And nothing in this world is lonelier."

Then as we watched the party on the hill,
"If you still wish to go there, give my name
And they will let you in; they did the same
To gain admittance and remain there still.
Champagne and stars are wonderful until
The whispering becomes a boring game;
No paradise unearned can ever claim
To satisfy our longings, or fulfill.
On that great lawn, the scattered lights are green,
The future that seduces you is there;
But you will find it shallow, and the cheer,
The music, laughter, dancing you have seen
Becomes a tiresome repetition where
The host himself will often not appear."

"They all believe that they are avant-garde;
But some had invitations, some did not,
Some gave a name or password, some forgot.
To enter? That was easy; exit? Hard.
And you, who felt uniquely so ill-starred
That you were kept excluded from that spot
May yet escape the paradise you sought
And gain a greater one that is unmarred.
The nightingales are captives in their cages,
The trout cannot escape their enclosed pond;
And those who passively enjoy euphoria
Soon find that endless life which disengages
From all outside itself and those beyond
Becomes a boring, false phantasmagoria."

I looked back to the massive house until
I saw it indistinctly, for it glowed
Through intervening mist, while music flowed
Unfocused with the laughter, down the hill.
The two of us were wet, the night was chill,
The candle was the only light that showed
His servant's cottage there beside the road;
He asked me in, and "Yes", I said, "I will."
The single modest room was very small,
And furnishings were likewise very few,
Remarkable for their austerity.
"It is not much", he said, "but it is all
That I possess, and I will share with you
Whatever you may need of what you see."

Although the fire was dying, still some heat
Extended through the single room, and yet
I radiated steam, my clothes were wet,
Contentment at the least was incomplete.
He found the only chair, gave me a seat
Beside the fire, as close as I could get,
With kindness that I will not soon forget;
And then he washed and dried and warmed my feet.
He brought me blankets while my clothes were drying,
Then raked the fire and offered me his dinner
Which hung above the flame, a single bowl
Impressing me as less than satisfying.
The soup was thin, and shared, was even thinner,
And yet it fed both body and the soul.

Then over time, my garments warmed and dried,
And wrapped within a blanket, so did I;
My host was reticent, as if to pry
Into my life was not yet justified.
But then my hunger started to subside,
I felt that I should try to clarify
The reason I was wandering and why
My entrance to the mansion was denied.
I started with my journey and the time
I spent with oracles and scientists,
With prophets and philosophers, all speaking
Important truths, both simple and sublime,
(A few were pious, some were humanists);
And then he asked what I was truly seeking.

By this, he meant examining the course
That I had followed blindly to this place,
Accepting what was given me with grace
But no true understanding of the source.
What I had heard would only re-enforce
The need I felt, but never could erase,
The memory within my inner space
Of life and love, and loss, and death's divorce.
So now I must remember and define
The purpose of my journey, what I sought
When I began, so very long ago,
And why of all opinions and divine
Illuminations I had seen, none brought
An answer or assurance I should know.

And so, I started slowly to retrace
My passages, and those whom I had met;
I saw them in my mind, did not forget
A single one, superb or commonplace,
The things they taught, which time would not erase.
Their differing opinions that offset
Each other signified to my regret
That I had not yet found a stable space.
I needed strength, and reasons not to roam;
There was no loss or sickness, death or danger
In that bright world to which I wished to go.
If there was nowhere I could call my home,
Then I, a poor and lost wayfaring stranger
Had confidence that he would tell me so.

At last, when I was silent, waiting so
That if he understood what I expressed
And had a sound perception of his guest
He would instruct, before I had to go,
In many things he knew, that I should know.
I thought his kindness when I was distressed,
The great serenity that he possessed
Must come from principles learned long ago.
I hoped for his humane consideration,
I sought his counsel for a regimen
That might be, for my life, a watershed.
Engaged in either prayer or meditation
He waited, looking inwardly, and then
He spoke to me, and this is what he said:

"Before the first beginning, there was light,
Authentic, pure and unadulterated,
As brilliant as it was disseminated,
And darkness could not overcome the sight.
You recognize your essence as finite
And so it is, the way it was created;
You wonder that your life is complicated
And worry that its end will be all right.
But look, I say, into beginnings where
There is a perfect equilibrium;
Soon your diverse distractions, now apart
Will re-unite, complete the circle, there
The *two* will be as *one* and overcome
Confusion with a peace within your heart."

"There is no realm of fire, nor one of air,
And likewise not a hemisphere of land
Nor one of water; we must understand
That cavities of Hell exist somewhere
But not beneath the earth. We are aware
That no divine designer ever planned
A universe as intricate and grand
As Dante's manifold descending stair.
The Circles of Inferno and the Ledges
Of Purgatory and the Correspondence
Of Paradise are all imaginary,
To illustrate the center and the edges
Of virtue, vice, elation and despondence,
Of God Himself and of His adversary."

"The poets and the prophets who assess
The planets (some within but most beyond
The shadow of the earth) to correspond
To human deprivation or excess
Of qualities of strength or wickedness
Or virtues, lined up neatly, echeloned,
Compose a false imaginary bond;
Their moral universe is meaningless.
The peaceful kingdom will at last be found
Not in the heavens, nor a distant star
Nor any universe that laws control,
But in a realm far greater, more profound,
So deep within ourselves and what we are
That paradise is in the human soul."

"Let one who searches never cease to seek,
Until he finds the truth that is surrounded
By radiating light, and is astounded,
Perplexed and troubled that it is unique.
With new awareness, he begins to speak
To those around him, who have been confounded
By sophistry and arguments that sounded
Confused as if composed in ancient Greek.
But then the modern prophets say to you
'The Kingdom of our God is in the sky';
If so, the nightingales were there before.
If 'in the sea' the trout will be in view,
But both are out of reach; the dragonfly
Will hover out of range forevermore."

"The Kingdom is within you, and outside,
For lights within a lantern radiate
And all can see, for they illuminate
A path that in the night is clarified.
Thus you must know yourself and be a guide
To all who live in darkness and await
The beacons that will truly indicate
Salvation that the prophets have implied.
If you bring forth the light that is within you
What you bring forth will be your sparing grace,
And everything in life will over-joy you.
If you are seeking truth, you must continue,
For this if shared, will be a holy space,
But if you keep it hidden, will destroy you."

"A city that is sited on a hill
And lit and fortified cannot be taken,
Nor is it ever hidden or forsaken
But through the night remains a beacon still.
No lantern lit is able to fulfill
Its mission if when ready it is shaken
So that the flame goes out, nor re-awaken
Beneath a basket on a window-sill.
But in its proper place upon a stand
Whoever comes or goes will see its light,
And all the house will be illuminated.
Your eyes are such a lamp, and can expand
Your influence to those within your sight,
And all will be inspired, and liberated."

"But how should you achieve this living state
Of inner peace and grace, illumination?
Not by withdrawal, self-renunciation
Nor liturgies, which only abdicate
The duty and the charge to germinate
Within your soul an inner revelation
Of principles that lead to transformation;
Integrity is what you must create.
Do not tell lies to any other man,
Nor to yourself, all pretense is forbidden.
Your honor will be crushed if you continue
In any way to be a charlatan.
However deeply it is veiled or hidden,
The gift, of truth discovered, is within you."

"Above all else, escape hypocrisy
But have no rancor for the ones who lie,
For though you speak the truth and verify
Your thoughts and words, there is no guarantee
That you are virtuous as you should be.
Removing slivers from your brother's eye
Is simpler if you first identify
And then cast out your own deficiency.
The Pharisees and scholars have forbidden
Your access to the keys of knowledge, which
Would liberate the one who truly loves
Perfection and integrity, have hidden
The clues away in order to be rich.
Be wise as serpents, innocent as doves."

"Live modestly and not beyond your means
For wealth and riches have no valuation
Or worth outside of your imagination;
There are no Scriptures that embody scenes
Of gates to heaven lined with limousines.
And no amount of pious adoration
Will compensate for moral degradation,
There is no blessed place for libertines.
You ask about the ones who, merely rich,
Lead otherwise productive, sober lives,
But do not share, consumed with selfishness?
Already they have chosen courses which
Are like a party, where a guest arrives
To find the gathering is meaningless."

"It has been said, 'Lend not at interest,
Nor calculate the money you could earn,
But give it to the poor, without return',
For those who gave away what they possessed,
The generous, compassionate, are blessed.
The buyer and the merchant both must learn
(Together with the rich), that though they yearn
To enter Heaven, they will be hard-pressed.
The world you see outside is upside-down,
For he who *has* the least, but understands
The force of Love, and lives accordingly
Will merit paradise, and great renown.
So give the world no more than it demands,
Reserve the rest for God and charity."

"True charity is like a porous sieve,
Through which your gifts will flow as easily
As light will pass the other way, and be
A revelation of the way you live.
Do not expect re-payment when you give,
But know that all true generosity
Keeps no accounts, needs no apology;
It stands alone, itself definitive.
Be generous whenever you are rich,
When you are poor, still somewhat generous;
Contribute just as much as you are able.
There is great value in the efforts which
Will help (though they are inconspicuous)
The work of others that they may enable."

"You must desist from *preaching* righteousness
Until you find a solid cornerstone
Of moral, upright life that is your own,
If not, your eloquence is meaningless.
For there are hypocrites who will profess
A perfect virtue that is theirs alone,
But have no stable grounding, have not shown
The moral bedrock we must all possess.
Do not pursue salvation *from* this world,
But virtue *in* your life while you are here;
This will allow a total disregard
For darkness into which you might be hurled.
And then you will not need to live in fear,
Your righteousness will be its own reward."

"Be just and fair, unprejudiced to all,
For justice comes from virtue, from the heart.
Equality for all, a vital part
Of moral systems, creates ethical
And democratic standards which forestall
A biased attitude, which would then start
A downward spiral, setting some apart
For rectitude or sin, to rise or fall.
For what conforms unto the Law of God
Is just for all, and none are left behind,
And none are placed immune upon a shelf.
The ranks of men, the even and the odd
Are equal in the Law, and so your mind
Must also see each person as yourself."

"The ancient Laws are full of prohibitions
Concerning what one can or cannot do,
And things one must not eat, as if they knew
The ultimate in moral definitions.
But you who go to strangers, or on missions
Must never treat their customs as taboo,
Should eat whatever they may serve to you,
And heal the sick among them, as physicians.
For what goes in your mouth will not defile
Your cleanliness, nor cause an evil state,
It is to God an optional convention.
Compassion in your heart, to reconcile,
To pacify and to accommodate
Is far more virtuous than is abstention."

"To live in harmony with all mankind
Is fine to *say*, but somewhat hard to *do*.
But if you firmly wish this to be true,
Your life should be so constantly refined,
Each moment your behavior re-aligned,
That you can say you did the best you knew;
Or treat all others as they should treat you,
The ultimate is with the two combined.
Awareness is the key, for you must love
Your brother like your self, protecting him.
Make use of both your eyes, do not forsake
The light that fills us all from far above,
And keeps our spirits from becoming dim;
Be sensitive to others, stay awake."

"No man can mount two horses, bend two bows,
No servant serve two masters, there must be
An insight and a firm priority,
For when one door is opened, one will close.
And most unfortunate of all are those
Who cannot choose their path decisively,
Distinguish what is real from fantasy
And walk serenely in the way they chose.
The world in which we live contains distractions
Diverse or centered, some that we create;
Examine these, you can identify
The ones that cause you great dissatisfactions.
Dismiss them from your mind, and concentrate,
For in this life, we all are passers-by."

"There is no integral dichotomy
Between ourselves and our creative Source,
Nor from each other, nor is there divorce;
Apparent separations are the key
To all our guilt, unnatural debris
Disordering our lives, they re-enforce
Destructive actions, that within their course
Impair God's virtue and His harmony.
Reject the world's inhibiting distractions,
Encumbrances to seeing something real,
Forget imagined sin and expiation,
Return to innocence and truth in actions;
Condense the two of these in one ideal,
And this will be your spirit's consummation."

"There is no profit in assigning blame
For things that are unfortunate or mean,
Occurrences with motives byzantine
And devious, corrupt, or which inflame
The cycle of the claim and counter-claim.
To work for peace and to remain serene
Confronting violence, to intervene
With kindness and concern are all the same.
These indicate compassion, universal,
Unlimited, extending to all men,
And fitting every moral situation.
Each minor incident is one rehearsal
That will occur again and yet again,
Until it culminates in revelation."

"Then what will be revealed to you is this:
The Laws of God are those of affirmation,
Of true equality within creation;
Inside the Law, no creature is amiss,
Permitting not the slightest prejudice.
And therefore, to evaluate or judge
Another person, or to hold a grudge
Is wrong, and will become your nemesis.
But more than merely passively forgiving
Apparent difference, we must proclaim
In everything we do, and all we say
An active, equal role in all of living.
And if you think, 'They will not do the same,'
My answer is, *to do it anyway*."

"If you find moral laws to be diffuse
Or negative, (as in the admonitions
Of ancient codes containing prohibitions),
Or in their finished form, they are abstruse
And you would like to simplify, reduce,
Consolidate, without a great omission
But still have clarity, your intuition
Will lead you to these standards for your use:
It has been said that there are only four
Essential qualities of Godly lives,
And they are faith and hope and memory
And generosity; and at the core,
The central one, from which all else derives,
A constant love for all humanity."

"Both memory and hope are secondary;
For one, extending back into the past
Has this restriction: that it will not last,
Its life in time is only momentary,
Then it will die with us. The visionary
Anticipation of a wish forecast
May never happen, or may be out-classed
By other dreams, as facts make necessary.
And faith, the evidence of things not seen,
Is part of every life, but only part,
For no one knows if it is justified.
A multitude of things can intervene
Between the place we end, and where we start,
And thus we should in present time reside."

"To be in present time is to exist
Without regard for what has gone before,
Or what is yet to come, and not deplore
The opportunities you may have missed.
You need not preach like an evangelist;
Your generosity will underscore
The loving-kindness that is yet the core,
The soul, the heart of every altruist.
But charity cannot exist alone;
Specific acts are all affirmative,
And as a principle throughout your lives
They represent a key, a cornerstone.
Yet this itself is still derivative
And only through a greater force survives."

"And so, more central, there is yet another
Essential rule of living, more complete,
That renders all the others obsolete.
You honor both your father and your mother,
Then growing in maturity, your brother,
And finally the stranger that you meet
Informally, or in the open street;
There is one single standard: Love each other.
'And those', you ask, 'who will not love you back?'
Or those unpleasant, lacking any charm,
The ignorant, embarrassing, risqué,
The proud and foolish egomaniac,
The argumentative, who truly wish you harm?
I say to you, *to love them anyway*."

"So do these things: be honest, do not lie,
And give the world your best, and willingly;
Commit to concord and serenity,
In times of conflict, try to pacify.
Concede that some are devious and sly,
Forgive their blindness and discourtesy;
Be kind to all without apology,
And generous, without a reason why.
Do good to all, and build, do not destroy;
No wickedness is insurmountable,
If you love those who in their turn condemn,
You still can have contentment, peace and joy.
To God alone you are accountable,
It never was between yourself and them."

"So let the light that is within you shine,
Illuminating all the world outside;
So that your life, which seems diversified,
Divided now, will once again combine
Into a singleness which will align
The things within and those without, and guide
These emanations, so that they provide
A Harmony which surely is divine.
Then there will be no longer a division
Of categories or a dualism,
No good or evil, black or white or red,
No body versus soul, or a transition
From life to death and no antagonism
Of heaven, hell, the living and the dead."

I looked into a mirror on his wall
And indistinct but true, I saw my face
As it was now, it did not quite replace
But overlaid an image I recall
From long ago, when I was young and tall;
And even more, I thought I saw a trace:
Myself, but in a state of perfect grace,
Not knowing anything of life at all.
Then light was in the window, in the house,
The night was gone and I was satisfied,
And dressed and warm, stepped out into the road.
A fluttering of early morning grouse,
A single hawk in long and silent glide
Announced the ending of this episode.

My host and I were standing near the fence.
"The gate is closed, but if you still desire,
It can be opened, know however, prior
To entering these grounds, the consequence:
One never leaves, the shallow opulence
Which bright naïve novitiates admire
Will prove itself a hypocrite and liar,"
But I declined this whole experience.
We marveled how this wealth had come to dwell
In places of such moral poverty.
Displays of superficial elegance,
Like painted horses on a carousel
Were mindless, unaware, a fallacy;
What some called sin was only ignorance.

That incoherent failure of a mansion
Stood silently, alone, and I forgot
The fathomless emotional expansion
That some could feel while there, but I could not.
Then, one-by-one the window-lights went out,
The contours of that gorgeous house grew dim,
Reality itself was now in doubt
As if the solid stones had been a whim.
The lawn had disappeared into the night,
The hill was empty and the building gone,
As if an early traveler now might
Endeavor to return to Babylon.
The lack of ruins sharpened my conclusion:
That all that had been there was mere illusion.

But there remained one lone reality,
A single figure standing in the road
And waiting, looking at me patiently,
Remaining for the final episode.
His offer was to stay and be with him,
For he had shown me all that I must do
To see the beacon that would never dim
And know an equal truth to what he knew.
But I had learned the secret, hidden key
Unlocking life itself, the central way
From hopelessness to peace and ecstasy.
The dawn had come at last, I could not stay,
For I had far to go before I slept,
And many promises that must be kept.

THE PROPHET

Then swift, as summoned by a sorcerer,
I saw a rider, mounted and descending,
A cavalier beyond my comprehending
On winged horse, celestial traveler.
And when he reached the earth, this voyager
Approached me rapidly, as if intending
To interrupt my course, then said, unbending,
"My name is Gabriel, the messenger".
He sat upon his stallion, in the mist
And told me of his mission, to transmit
The holy revelations, told in stages.
To oracles he was the catalyst
That brought the sacred Light, and then who lit
The lamps within the prophets, through the ages.

"I brought God's will to Abraham, to Mary,
That they should show the ultimate submission;
To slay a son, to bear a son, fruition
Of God's own plan requires a voluntary
Surrender of one's self. The corollary
Would be that one should never have ambition
That he alone, of personal volition
Could create any holy sanctuary.
To Zachariah and Elizabeth
I brought the news that they would have a son,
Although they were convinced their time was past.
When Daniel's vision of our life and death
Required analysis, I brought him one;
And now, another prophet, this the last."

He swept me up behind him on his steed
(To such an angel, one cannot say "No"),
And though our flight gave rise to vertigo,
I had resolved to seek where he would lead.
Our destination never guaranteed,
The distance limitless, yet far below
I saw that we traversed a vast plateau
With valleys and with ridges filigreed.
And then there was a mountain with a cave;
Inside we found a man who, meditating,
Was certainly the one for whom we came.
He greeted us with courtesy, forgave
The interruption, stood, anticipating,
And as he rose, the angel said "Proclaim."

He spoke, at first reverberating bells,
Enchanting and compelling and which spread
To tintinnabulation in my head,
And everywhere to deep hypnotic spells.
In these, a deep receptive state compels
Attention, not to senses, but instead
To revelations, words that would be said,
"Proclaim the faith, awaken infidels."
Within the cave, the angel's radiance
Had shone upon a man who was arising
In salutation, but when bells were heard,
And then the message, slipped into a trance;
For he was concentrating, memorizing
The statement of the angel, every word.

On this, the Night of Power, all creation
And all of nature sensed a certain peace.
It turned toward God, and time appeared to cease,
While he who waited in anticipation
Without distraction, open to sensation,
Could hear the trees grow tall, the grass increase;
And when his soul was open, found release
To feel the clarity of revelation.
Within this holy space the angel spoke,
"I brought the same command to Samuel,
To Moses, Jesus, and to Solomon,
To Abraham, and each of them awoke,
Receiving messages that would compel
Renewal as a holy paragon."

"Again, I bring the same command to you:
Inert and wrapped within your cloak, arise,
Awake in wonder, do not agonize,
But hear the words of God, transmitted through
An angel's voice, commandments that are true.
You must not question these, nor criticize
But understand, go out, evangelize,
Proclaim to all the Word of God anew."
Then, though he claimed he could not testify,
The angel held him in a firm embrace,
Until, now helpless, he could not control
His natural resistance to comply;
For I could tell, by changes in his face,
The angel's words were branded on his soul.

"The God existed at the genesis,
Creating first the world, then living things,
Those of the earth, the sea, and those with wings,
With nothing fragmentary or amiss.
Nor was there bigotry or prejudice
Or evil thoughts or any sufferings
But only perfect dazzling wakenings,
An excellent and flawless edifice.
You cannot find, in all The God's creation
An imperfection, if you try to gaze,
Then you would find it blinding to your sight.
The ultimate of your imagination
Conceives of only that which will amaze,
Illuminated by His holy light."

"Proclaim your sovereign Lord who has created
All human forms from stone and syntheses,
With blood and moving water, both of these
With breath from blowing wind are integrated.
Humanity was made, articulated
From perfect elements, this guarantees
Its nature to be good and thus to please
The God whose work is thereby consummated.
Do not allow demand for miracles
And mystic signs to lead you from your task,
Proclaim your Lord, most generous, most true;
For God alone removes all obstacles,
He answers every question you might ask,
And teaches men the things they never knew."

"Through God's own grace you will be satisfied;
Whenever you may lift your heart and soul
Into His presence He will make you whole.
No imperfection ever can reside,
Nor blind and heedless unawareness hide
Within the infinite informed control
Of all the universe, and of His role
As guardian and shelterer and guide.
Thus, from His mercy comes a world of joy,
With air and sun and light and confidence
And knowledge, what is wrong and what is right,
These are the things that sin cannot destroy;
There is reward for moral excellence,
And pardon for the ones who are contrite."

"By noon-day sun or darkness of the night,
Your Lord forsakes you not, is not displeased;
The demons of your life have been appeased
And troubles of the past now set aright.
For He can understand your present plight:
Anxiety with which you all are seized,
But will, as torments of today are eased
Convert distress to ultimate delight.
Did He not find you, lonely, wandering,
An orphan, constantly condemned to roam?
As always, He was bounteous and true.
When you were poor and needy, sorrowing,
He did enrich, provide for you a home,
When you were lost and straying, guided you."

"There is no innate sin in God's creation,
And none in you by pure inheritance,
But all are prone at times to arrogance,
Forgetting that their soul's divine foundation
Is worthy of an endless adoration.
Resulting from this careless ignorance
Are lives of constant moral dissonance,
With want of gratitude and affirmation.
The infidel lacks faith and thankfulness,
A traveler through life both deaf and blinded
Who cannot see or hear, cannot connect
To God, the source of power, limitless.
They need to be corrected and reminded
In order to regain their self-respect."

"The God, invisible, cannot be seen,
(Because of this, cannot be represented).
He is the Ultimate, unprecedented,
Replacing idols from the sacred scene.
And being universal and serene
The God in stature cannot be augmented,
And in His stillness never discontented,
In power infinite, in peace pristine.
He has no common human attributes;
To say you are His children is a thing
That is not proper, for comparison
Of our restrictions with His absolutes
Shows arrogance beyond imagining,
The God of mercy never had a son."

"Within the House of God are many splendors,
Some you have seen, but some you have not known;
Of all of these the crucial cornerstone
Is absolute commitment, which engenders
The peace which comes when all your life surrenders
Completely, willingly, to God alone.
This giving of one's self, of all you own
Must be complete, God notices pretenders.
He knows the sum within the land and sea,
And all the mysteries of life and death,
Dishonesty is always disbelieved.
You need not raise your voice pretentiously,
For He is truly closer than your breath,
And knows your secret whisper, undeceived.

"The many stages of God's revelation
Began with Abraham and recognition
Of God as One, without an opposition,
And with no rivals or divine relation.
This God, responsible for all creation,
Was indivisible by definition,
And everlasting, whole without attrition,
And will be so until the world's salvation.
The vision that began with Abraham
Was carried on by prophets of the Jews
Throughout the centuries, until the present.
The statement without question was 'I am';
And whether we believe or we refuse,
The image in itself is incandescent."

"So that His people knew how they should live,
God sent through Moses ethical directions,
Commandments to correct their imperfections,
A righteous and a strict imperative.
But then, like water through a porous sieve,
The people found the loopholes, with objections
That complicated codes were mere collections
Of limitations they could not forgive.
A new and binding covenant was needed,
And therefore God sent Jesus to unite
The many Laws into a single one.
And this He did; and in one rule succeeded
In summarizing what God said was right,
Completing what the prophets had begun:"

" 'To love your God with all your heart and soul
And equally to love your fellow man',
(Profound as any thought since time began,
Simplicity and truth were both a goal).
This noble Golden Rule was, as a whole
Sublime, but also called for the Quran
For final revelation of God's plan;
Mohammed (peace be with him) fills this role.
No greater prophets ever came before,
And none will in the future follow him;
The others were authentic, no illusion,
But incomplete, as if to underscore
The need for one beyond an interim,
The Seal of all the prophets, their conclusion."

"To every one God gives a law and way;
Each person has a voluntary will
Responsible for good or evil, still
What God commands, all people must obey.
Now granted, there are some who go astray,
And some who over good may choose the ill,
Existing blindly, carelessly until
Their lives are shown to be in disarray.
He could have made one faith if He believed
That all should be alike, but He did not.
To everyone He sent a messenger,
Which some accepted, others felt deceived;
A few have listened once (and then forgot),
Or sought a way they thought was easier."

"There should be no compulsion to believe,
For God will judge each one of you alone,
According to the insight you have shown
And what, within this framework, you achieve.
So press on forward with good works and leave
To God the right to censure or condone,
For each will reap whatever he has sown;
To judge another is at best naïve.
Why would you force compliance and belief
On unenlightened people, since you know
That all things came from God, and only He
Bestows upon each person joy or grief.
When you return to Him, then He will show
Solutions to the ways you disagree."

"When suns are folded up, the stars will fall,
And even mountains will be set in motion;
When seas are swept away into the ocean,
Then every life is proved ephemeral.
For in its brief and precious interval
It had a single chance for true devotion;
Yet many are distracted by commotion
As if the Peace of God is optional.
Then every soul will know what it has done,
And where it stands on scales of righteousness.
The contrast of the heavens and the hells
Reveals a critical comparison;
On one hand are the lives that God will bless,
And on the other, faithless infidels."

"The vital elements within each prayer,
Include our homage, praise and gratitude,
In which allegiance is affirmed, renewed.
For every mortal person must declare
His attitude, elation or despair,
His confidence, or fears that may intrude,
And how he plans to spend this interlude,
This time, this gift of God, unique and rare.
The God is God, and there is nothing greater,
You live within the world that He has made,
Appreciate your standing, when you pray
Give praise unto The God, the One Creator,
Be open to His mind and ask His aid;
This is the way, and these the things you say."

"To walk a path which, absolutely straight,
Leads from the place you find yourself today,
Without distortion, through a passageway
To God, the Merciful, Compassionate;
This is the effort that will generate
A prospect to be viewed without dismay,
But not the path of those who go astray,
And wander, lost, confused, disconsolate.
The way of righteousness is just, direct,
Explicit in the things that all should know,
And clear to those who look to Him for grace.
Of Paradise, He is the architect,
He guides us in the way that we must go,
That night and morning, we may see His face."

"When life has been a gift from its Creator,
A natural response is one of fear
Of power which is infinite, its sphere
Encompassing the universe, and greater
Because of strict morality. A straighter
Uncompromising path could not appear
To guide your lives; if you are insincere,
Then God Himself will be your arbitrator.
Thus you must show respect and thankfulness
In place of fear, for all your life is due
To one dynamic matching His design.
This duty recognizes limitless
Allegiance to His moral law, and to
The peace which faithfulness and trust define."

"A second obligation is submission,
A total and complete commitment to
The Will of God; by this surrender you
Will free yourself from pride and from ambition.
Then greed, unhealthy drive for acquisition
Will be transformed, without a residue,
And reconstructed, changed into a new
Authentic charity without condition.
Allow the bounty of your life to flow
Without self-seeking, through yourself and on;
To hoard the gift of God (unnatural
As hiding blessings which He will bestow),
Deserves disparagement, comparison
To fools who seek to dam a waterfall."

"Complete surrender means to be a slave
To God and love, and thereby to be freed
From other forms of slavery: from greed,
Extravagant desire for things you crave,
From striving that can cause you to behave
With arrogance to others, and impede
Humility, which all of us will need
To balance blunders which The God forgave.
Anxiety, which at its worst is fear
Will be the consequence of your defiance;
Refusal to surrender and commit
Unto the will of God, and to adhere
To ill-considered total self-reliance,
Are hallmarks of a foolish hypocrite."

"The soul is individual and free,
Responsible to God, each one unique,
Controlling its own fate, what it may seek,
Achieving its distinctive destiny.
This personal potential certainly
May demonstrate an essence, strong or weak
That brings to each an outcome bright or bleak
Consistent with its moral purity.
Fulfillment of the spirit thus depends
On faithful mindfulness and constant prayer,
Conformity to God's own doctrinal
Instruction, and the way the soul transcends
Its limitation and becomes aware
That God Himself is individual."

"Whoever dwells in sin and goes astray
Is solely and alone responsible
For all his actions, for each obstacle
Between himself and God, a castaway
Who wanders through the chaos of each day
Without a center, life a spectacle
Of futile errors, all of which annul
Directives of The God we must obey.
But this elicits one great mystery,
For God, omnipotent, can do whatever
He knows is good, the universe evolved
According to His perfect plan, and we
Are likewise destined; this enigma never
In all of history has been resolved."

"But those who earned His wrath and went astray,
Must know the vivid images of hell;
For death will burn away the citadel
Of self-defense which served to keep away
The hard but honest truth that underlay
The actions of their lives, it will compel
A reckoning wherein they say farewell
To hidden secrets of corrupt decay.
Some human actions are by God forbidden,
But others are declared obligatory,
And some are minor, or indifferent.
The principles for these no longer hidden,
Each action fits a certain category,
With judgment on the whole now evident."

"The Jewish and the Christian Testaments
(Both Old and New) are valid affirmations
That God is One, and sending revelations
Attesting to His great benevolence.
They certify with faithful eloquence
To holy covenants and demonstrations
Of His great strength and love through His creations,
The universe and all its excellence.
The Torah and the Gospels are the bridge
Into the last disclosure of God's will,
The People of the Book are all devout.
The early Scriptures are your heritage,
Which this, your recitation, shall fulfill
And is the Word, whereof there is no doubt."

"The Jewish Law is narrow, meant for them,
Their *Yahweh* is the God of Israel;
This vision, though, remains your sentinel,
The image of the root, the trunk, the stem
Of God whose name is both a synonym
For righteousness (and also parallel
To unity and peace), but is as well
A God whose name is plural, *Elohim*.
The prophet, Jesus, tried to simplify
The labyrinth of rules within the Law;
His principle of love is not exceeded
By any faith one can identify.
And yet there is one all important flaw,
A further explication now is needed."

"The other Jewish prophets, Solomon,
And Moses and Isaiah lived a long
Complete career; whenever they were wrong
God spoke to them, their testament went on.
Not so with Jesus, by comparison,
His ministry was both intense and strong,
But one which even He could not prolong;
A mere three years, and all His work was done.
Because of this, His role was incomplete,
(He found the key of Love, not how to use it);
Despite the eloquence of all His preaching,
The One who sits upon the Judgment Seat
Concerned that man might misconstrue, abuse it,
Required a final witness to His teaching."

"In daily life, compassion is the prime
And over-riding guide to every action.
There is, before The God, no clique or faction,
The *highly praised* the only paradigm.
The peasant and the peddler spend their time
As well as do the rich in interaction
With all the brotherhood, for no abstraction
Denies that loving-kindness is sublime.
The poorest of the poor have dignity
Arising from a common confidence
That all are equal, prince and publican;
The path will not allow antipathy
Between the travelers, the eminence
Belongs to God, and not to any man."

"The God has said to you, 'Pray constantly,
Or fifty times (or more) each waking day'.
But if you speak to Moses, he will say
That no one here on earth can possibly
Invest the time that this requires, and he
Was quite familiar with the people's way,
Their short attention span; a few will stay
In constant prayer, but most will disagree.
So my advice is this: *negotiate*,
And see if God will be more flexible,
Allowing all the people now alive
To spend less of their time, in aggregate,
In worship; it would be a miracle
If daily prayers are ever more than five."

(And so it was, five times in every day;
The God allowed the Prophet to insist
That this was quite enough, and would consist
Of such devotion that the disarray
Of common daily life would go away,
And leave perspective that would co-exist
With order, confidence they would have missed
Without the obligation thus to pray.
The cleansing of the body and the soul
In preparation for the pure communion
Of man and God distinctly indicates
That only those who, clean and in control
Of all their lives approach the mystic union,
The harmony man seeks, God consecrates.)

"A certain part of all your wealth each year
Must willingly be given to the poor;
A small or moderate expenditure,
A generosity that is sincere,
May ease existences that are austere.
The wealthy have a duty to ensure
That all who live are basically secure,
For poverty will never disappear.
Which one of you is destined to be rich?
How many will emerge less fortunate?
And how is providence distributed?
Each person occupies a certain niche
By luck or fortune more than honest sweat;
Your means may fade, and leave you poor instead."

"Yet all on earth are equal in the eyes
Of their Creator on a moral plane,
According to the virtue they attain
By their integrity, and how they rise
In gratitude and praise and otherwise
The life they live, how holy and humane,
Their quality of faith, how they sustain
Allegiance to The God they recognize.
But virtue does not translate easily
To fortune, as in wealth which some inherit,
To those, unworthy, who by chance are rich.
The ones who *have* must share it graciously
With those in need, but who have equal merit,
Thus you must fill your role, and you know which."

"And as you make your life-long pilgrimage,
Remind yourself of man's equality,
Regardless of his wealth or penury,
Discounting any ancient lineage
(And equally an unknown parentage;
Before your Lord there is no bastardy).
The honest poor inherit clemency,
And only virtue merits leverage.
Thus entry into Paradise depends
On qualities within the range of all,
For every one can rise to high accord
Where honor, moral righteousness, transcends
The signs of social status; integral
Are prince and beggar, equal in the Lord."

"And once each year the faithful must commence
An austere and a rigid regimen,
A time of added moral discipline,
A month of fasting, prayer and abstinence.
Through self-denial they experience
A heightened clarity, a crystalline
Perception of their frailty, wherein
Their trust in God is rendered more intense.
And fasting also magnifies compassion
By showing some, the richer and the younger
Conditions they will meet when they are old;
Denial serves the spirit in this fashion,
They feel the wretched state produced by hunger,
And are inspired to ease what they behold."

"Once in their lives, each person must return
To their religious home, their origin,
Declare allegiance to The God again,
Receiving reassurance as they learn
Of His immense commitment and concern.
There is no rank or difference in men
Who stand before the Lord in genuine
Devotion, or the prize that they will earn.
Humanity is undivided here,
With none above another or apart,
But all are equal in obedience.
The faithful pilgrim who remains sincere
And holds the Word of God within his heart
Will be rewarded for his diligence."

"And now you have been told what you must do
To earn the favor, harmony, accord
Between yourselves and with your sovereign Lord;
The essence here can be condensed into
The principles that Jesus said were true:
'To love each other, shunning all discord,
But first to love your God', and your reward
Will be the greatest peace you ever knew.
There also are some things that are forbidden,
A prototype of these, the Law of Moses
On which is based your code and recitation.
The Laws of God are open, never hidden,
To every one who listens, God discloses
The rules of moral life and their foundation."

"A righteous war must be in your defense
Or else to right a wrong or injury,
Thus you avoid the sin, hypocrisy.
For war will come, but let the evidence
Reveal the reason for the violence
To be a holy cause; duplicity
And hatred lead to moral anarchy,
Intention is the crucial difference.
Between the concepts, justice versus mercy
There is eternal tension, constant strife;
Do not attack, instead forgive a debtor,
Abstain from all un-called for controversy.
Suppress internal anger in your life,
From evil, turn away toward what is better."

"But do not be so passive, or so blind
That you ignore overt hostility.
External evil must, accordingly,
Be challenged, and when properly defined,
Resisted and opposed, or undermined.
In order to restore the harmony
And righteousness which is your legacy
Defy iniquity of every kind.
The punishment of wanton sinners will
Be equal to the injury they cause.
Defend yourself against your enemies;
Do not attack them first but wait until
Necessity is clear, for God withdraws
Approval from aggressors such as these."

"But times will come when justice will demand
Resistance to corruption in return;
The first imperative is to discern
If any lesser means are close at hand,
Such as diplomacy or reprimand.
In certain cases, amnesty will earn
A peaceful resolution; some will spurn
Accepting good for evil, as you planned.
Extend this justice to society
And you may see *jihad*, a holy war.
The canons of the blessed sacred way
Must be defended, always faithfully,
For righteous warfare is dissimilar
From selfish, brutal strife as night from day."

"The greatest holy war, the great exertion
Must be against the evil in your heart,
For this endeavor is the counterpart
Of struggle with extraneous perversion.
And those who demonstrate their self-assertion,
Fore-seeing and resisting from the start
Become revered and set themselves apart,
Examples of awareness and conversion.
Reborn into a state of consciousness,
They know themselves and how they must relate
To principles they never can achieve;
And yet they strive, and never acquiesce
To lesser levels that may fascinate
But never can express what they believe."

The angel, finished with the recitation
Was silent now, and all the cave was still.
The Prophet then repeated words until
He reached perfection, no exaggeration
And no omission; my approximation
Can only summarize, perhaps distill
The essence of the angel's message, fill
The central space within his affirmation.
"Do not be troubled that your life may cease,
Approval also comes to those who wait."
Before we left the cave I heard him say:
"May blessings be upon you, holy peace,
For God is One, and more than merely great;
There is no God but God, arise and pray."

Then he who was to be so highly praised
Throughout the world, was lost in ecstasy.
He heard the angel, and he was amazed,
Aware at last of God's great mystery.
He had alone been charged with words of weight,
Important far beyond imagination,
That altered him into a special state,
A sacred and unconscious transformation.
And then the angel from the cave retreated,
The Night of Power, concluded, now was closed.
The Prophet from his memory repeated
The words the angel spoke, but God composed.
But I was now secure in my decision,
And left him there, together with his vision.

THE RABBI AND PHYSICIAN

At Sabbath noon, the rabbi welcomed me
And told me that he had a little space,
A little only, for he must displace
Petitioners and patients, family,
And those concerned with immortality.
It seemed the whole Judaic populace
And many members of another race
Had gathered to discuss theology.
For only on the Sabbath could he find
The time to fit debate and study in.
His specialty, prevention of disease,
Made him (with skill in medicine combined),
Physician to the son of Saladin;
He was the great medieval Jew, Maimonides.

His theologic range was catholic,
From zealous Christian to barbarian;
He studied both the Talmud and Koran
And wrote in Hebrew and in Arabic.
But still, in writing and in rhetoric
He centered on the Torah, and began
And ended in the Law, that talisman
That split the Righteous from the heretic.
But even now he graciously consented
To teach, instruct, and help me understand
The essence of the faith that through dispersal
Had kept alive the Law that represented
Their hope, their promise of a Holy Land,
A kingdom that would yet be universal.

"The Pentateuch is beautiful, complex,
Six hundred thirteen precepts of the Law;
But for your needs it has one major flaw:
The web of intersecting rules may vex
The traveler, and even could perplex
The careful student, who might then withdraw
To simpler, lesser pieties; I saw
This danger, and I offered an annex.
I took the many precepts and condensed
Their multitude to thirteen principles.
So that a pilgrim, seeker, who would look
Into my summary, and referenced
The written Law, the first five chronicles,
Would never need consult another book."

"I called it 'Mishna Torah, Repetition',
Because it recapitulated all
The Laws that God had sent, in logical,
Concise and clearly reasoned definition.
I did allow myself just one omission,
Eliminating astrological
Talmudic regulation; overall,
I stayed within rabbinical tradition.
In place of many years of meditation
And study of the Scriptures and the Law,
I offer this to you; although it's brief,
It is a sound and valid condensation,
To help you understand, and think with awe
On Jewish revelation and belief."

But even *Mishna Torah* was too great,
Too long and too complex to understand;
Its thirteen principles of faith were planned
To simplify, condense, abbreviate
The Talmud, but remain subordinate.
And yet it grew into a work that spanned
Some thirteen books, all logical and grand,
Much more than I could ever contemplate.
The Rabbi offered me a substitute:
A condensation of his summary,
That Rabbi Daniel ben Yehudah wrote;
In thirteen verses, each would constitute
The essence of one principle that he
Derived from *Mishna Torah*, and would quote.

This poem, *Yigdal*, was liturgical,
And in translation, meant "Exalted be---".
The rabbi would recite it all to me,
Although it truly needed a chorale
That alternated in antiphonal
Replies; but he would try devotedly
To sing with all of his ability,
While we would walk, as in processional.
And so, we went together, synchronous
To metronomic rhythms of the chant,
And after he recited, I replied,
Until at last, by this vicarious
Participation in the covenant,
I almost felt my spirit sanctified.

"Exalted be the living God, and praised,
By all the priests and by the populace;
His presence can be felt in every place
But never be described or paraphrased.
Nor can His own existence be appraised;
Unbounded by the forms of time and space,
The will of God can easily erase
All limits that the mind of man has raised.
Our *Yahweh* pre-existed in His essence
The first creation, even that of light;
With just a single word He could disperse
The darkness and the chaos of the night,
And clarify with brilliant incandescence
The mysteries of all the universe."

"The essence of our God is Unity,
For He is One, and not divisible,
And nothing has been able to annul,
Diminish or divide his sanctity.
So infinite is His ascendency,
That He can pierce without an obstacle
The universal verge, the pinnacle
Where He has placed the farthest galaxy.
Inscrutable and uniform existence,
Cannot be probed by analytic thought;
In Oneness there can never be detection
Of qualities creating inconsistence,
Or features that are missing, but which ought
To be discovered for divine perfection."

"Since God is purest Spirit, nebulous,
No likeness or resemblance can be found
In human attributes, nor is He bound
By any of the laws that govern us.
The Word of God is not analogous
To any human speech, or even sound;
Thus all we know: that God is One, profound,
Whose essence is existence, glorious.
Nor can there be, to God's great holiness
A corresponding similarity;
He is a singular phenomenon.
For only God is able to compress
All holy attributes to Unity,
Eliminating all comparison."

"Before the moment of the first creation,
Preceding every being that was made,
And even prior to the first cascade
Of light that activated transformation
Of chaos into order, separation
Of earth from heaven with boundaries surveyed,
The will of God already was obeyed,
For God existed first in isolation.
Not even time itself was there before
The Mind of God began initial motion;
There was no space, no measurement or distance,
No substance, matter, and no central core
Or firmament dividing any ocean,
For nothing had preceded God's existence."

"There was a prophet once in history
Who clearly comprehended God's own vision;
Some others saw in parts, with imprecision,
But he alone could think inclusively.
He lived in unabridged conformity
To all the Law, and also could envision
A righteous life, so he, by God's decision
Was worthy of His Law and Prophecy.
And so, God gave to Moses, him alone,
The written evidence of His directive,
The tablets of the Law that he might hold,
And give to all the tribes, a cornerstone;
So Israelites, both single and collective,
Might see the Laws of which they had been told."

"The greatest gift that God could ever give
Was to bestow upon His Israel
The Law, the Torah (which could then dispel
The pagan superstitions, primitive
And dark, and holding truth much like a sieve
Holds water); it confronts the infidel,
Thus showing in a brilliant parallel,
The shining truth of God, and how to live.
And all this revelation came about
Because God's prophet, in his righteousness
Was trusted in the household of the Lord.
In congregations of the most devout,
Alone he was permitted to express
The Will of God, the ultimate accord."

"Behold, the Master of the universe
Is God, Creator and our sovereign,
For every being is a genuine
Creation; all the varied and diverse,
The tribes of men and creatures who disperse
Throughout the world, all draw their origin
From God, from whom still flows the discipline
In which each creature must itself immerse.
And God alone can prove and demonstrate
Eternal greatness and His sovereignty,
No others could through all recorded time
Approach His majesty or validate
A power equal to His energy;
Absorption in His glory is sublime."

"The gracious gift of God is prophecy,
Directed to the people He selected.
Whenever they were lost or disconnected,
He sent a prophet, voluntarily,
In order to correct their tendency
Toward independence and the unexpected
Indifference to Laws He had perfected;
Through prophets God extended amnesty.
Because to Him His people were a treasure,
And worth reminding of their special place,
He never disregarded or suspended
Observance of the Law, but His displeasure
Would never lead to their complete disgrace;
For in His sight, His people still were splendid."

"The Law contains no flexibility,
For God will neither change nor cancel it,
And any principle He may omit
Has some good reason that we may not see.
But God foresees with great validity
And therefore never needed to submit
Amendments or additions, or refit
His Law to changing customs, aimlessly.
And just as God will never rearrange
His Holy Law, but will preserve its truth
And purity to lead His chosen tribe,
For all eternity He will not change
A segment of the Law so that uncouth
Or gentile nations might in time subscribe."

"There is no secret hidden from God's eyes,
He scrutinizes all our hidden places;
And things we think forgotten, past disgraces,
Are as an open book we can't disguise,
Nor bury nor forget, nor minimize.
Our hearts and souls to Him are open spaces,
Which He can scan at will, and He retraces
The secret longings that we fantasize.
And God perceives a matter's outcome when
It has its very earliest inception.
He does not interfere, but can predict
How moral options will resolve, and then,
With absolutely crystalline perception,
The penalty the Law will thus inflict."

"God sends to virtuous humanity
His kindness in proportion to one's deeds,
And with Divine awareness always reads
The signs of generous philanthropy.
A righteous man, who lives in harmony
Will sense distress around him, so he heeds
The poverty of others, this precedes
Humane benevolence and clemency.
But woe unto the wicked in proportion
To sinfulness a life may demonstrate;
The consequences of hypocrisy,
Corruption or unscrupulous distortion
Of promises are stern and accurate,
But not as harsh as for idolatry."

"To those who long for ultimate salvation,
Be reassured, for God will not forget,
And even those with troubles, hard beset,
Take comfort in the safe anticipation:
Redemption is assured, the revelation
Of God unto His people is as yet
Unrealized, but certain to be met,
And bring the final reconciliation.
For by the End of Days, our God will send
Messiah, the anointed, holy One,
And He will liberate His people, those
Who keep the faith, and those who comprehend
That God will finish what He has begun,
Will not forsake the people that He chose."

"And those who die shall surely be revived,
In God's abundant kindness at the End.
Yet it is difficult to comprehend
How Islam (and Judaic thought) arrived
At Paradise, where bodies have survived
Intact, and for an extra dividend,
May live like Epicurus; I contend
That Heaven is only from the soul derived.
Creative, active *will* and intellect,
These gifts of God, immortal, are the part
That will survive our death and then reclaim
Perfection as it was, and intersect
In Unity with God, as at the start;
Forever blest be God's immortal Name."

When we had finished with this psalm of praise,
He said the essence of the Covenant
Contained within the verses of the chant
Was all I really needed to appraise
The Jewish faith and all its passageways
From man to God, and its concomitant
Requirements, rituals and elegant
Observance of the High and Holy Days.
To understand these details, intertwined,
Would be a wonderful accomplishment,
Yet take an endless study, and frustration.
"But you have found what you had come to find:
The essence of the Law and Testament,
And everything beyond is explanation."

The people of the Law and of the Book
Were singular within their confidence,
More certain than the ones that God forsook
Who wandered through the world in consequence,
Still seeking for the center of their life.
Unless they found it in another place
They were condemned to endless moral strife,
Suspended short of righteousness and grace.
And then I knew that this might be my fate;
As wondrous as the rabbi's song had been
One problem he could not alleviate:
I knew as soon as I had said "Amen",
I was not one of them, could never be,
How could their covenant apply to me?

JOURNEY'S END

HUMILITY AND GRACE

Then as I hurried on along my way,
A host of others called for my attention.
They almost were too numerous to mention,
And some were mystics, trying to convey
Their secret insight; some in strange array
Would whirl as if their dance was an extension
Of pious faith beyond my comprehension,
And some were prophets of a latter day.
Rejecting interaction some retreated,
Inviting me in silence to their prayers;
As if in isolation they would find
By contemplation, endlessly repeated
And chanted mantras, and their holy airs
The keys to life and heaven, intertwined.

Yet others stood on boxes near the road,
Proclaiming loudly the millennium
Which was at hand, and which would surely come
And be for some a fearful episode.
Still others spoke in tongues, perhaps in code;
Among them all, a pandemonium
Reverberated through the plain as some
Disputed others, and their tempers showed.
Fanatically, they strove to prophesy;
Despite their contradictory opinions
They offered me a mystic state of rapture,
Which would allow ascension to the sky,
Thereby escaping Satan and his minions,
Diminishing the prospects of my capture.

When I was young and had the time to spare,
I might have stayed and listened to whoever
Pretended to be confident and clever.
Those, brash as circus barkers, would declare
With loud conflicting clamor doctrinaire
Opinions, would entice one to endeavor
To win a prize which in the end would never
Result in true contentment, but despair.
With age, I lost that empty carefree space,
But gained awareness of simplicity.
I knew what I had learned and did not need
Confusion or conjectures to displace
The confidence that I had thoughtfully
Developed in a clear and honest creed.

So I escaped the great cacophony
Of hypocrites concerned for my salvation,
Who should themselves exchange their revelation
For something honest, with validity.
I felt that I already, painfully
Had reached a state of reasoned transformation,
The essence being partly moderation
Deriving from a self-autonomy.
But more than this, a deeper search had shown
A force, which ill-defined but dominant
Throughout the universe controlled our fate.
And I had journeyed through the world alone,
Approaching humbly, as a supplicant
Whoever might describe this steady-state.

There had been many who sincerely tried
(A few, I think, who consciously deceived);
I listened to them all, and I believed
In present time what I thought justified.
It had been true that some would over-ride
Another point of view, or had retrieved
Discredited opinions, or achieved
A fleeting eminence, which would subside.
For some had flaws that they could not conceal,
Fantastic dreams defying explanation,
Forgotten now, though once they thought they saw
Within their frame of reference a real,
A valid principle, an illustration
Of what became a universal law.

I heard a great profound beatitude,
And also some moronic prejudice,
A castle built on sand, an artifice
Of charlatans that passed for certitude.
But even as I watched, a multitude
Was drawn up to an edge, a precipice
That led to shining peaks or dark abyss
By searching thought, or shallow platitude.
When I had heard them all I then decided
Which ones to keep and which to throw away,
And which to save for later meditation.
I kept the ones that best defined and guided
A life that I could live and yet display
Serenity and honor, affirmation.

So I was finished seeking, and had found
Unique solutions to the quandaries
That I had faced so long ago; the keys
That seemed to serve me well, in truth were bound
To my distinct dilemmas (these surround
Each one of us with great anxieties,
But each one is unseen, the agonies
Are personal, encircling, tightly wound).
There now was nothing more for me to do
But find my way to where I had begun
And hope that someone lingered who would care.
I hurried, sometimes ran, and almost flew
Lest I, forsaken, lose what I had won;
Then I was safe, for she was waiting there.

This second time she motioned me to sit
Beside her on a single roughened stone;
So we were there together, quite alone
Where earth and wind and sky were infinite.
We sat in lengthy silence, opposite,
Both waiting; I, remembering the tone
With which she told me what I should have known,
Was wondering if she remembered it.
Her silence indicated expectation
That I would speak to her and summarize
Enlightenment I had experienced.
But she mistook the wordless concentration
I needed to condense and organize
My scattered thoughts, and therefore she commenced:

"To every exploration there will come
A time when all discovery is finished;
Then any further effort will succumb
To evidence, progressively diminished,
Which cannot satisfy, but just delay
Analysis, the closing contribution
To understanding what is true today
And lasts forever, final resolution.
The time has come that you alone review,
Evaluate the lessons you have learned,
Accept the principles you think are true,
Define yourself, the future you have earned.
Your search is done, its time for you to choose;
The prize is yours to win, or yours to lose."

This challenge made me focus, concentrate
And reach into the center of my soul
To find its essence, and condense its goal
Into a statement, brief but accurate.
I had the prophets to evaluate,
Their partisan devotion to control
And channel, synthesize, for on the whole
Not one alone was fully adequate.
So I reviewed my past experience,
The insight that each oracle presented,
The meanings of each statement, every term,
Evaluating them by common sense,
Selecting those with whom I felt contented,
And this, at last, is what I could affirm:

"In life, each person makes an affirmation
Of what one truly thinks, what one believes,
Distinctive from whatever one achieves
And separate from public declaration.
For deep within a soul, a dedication
Develops slowly, over time conceives
A basic central statement, one which leaves
No need for frivolous imagination.
Conviction, inwardly articulated,
Concise as possible, eliminating
Unnecessary words and other flaws,
Defines a life, both time now allocated
To being and existence, and awaiting
A correspondence with eternal laws."

"I cannot tell you whether God exists
But my belief will never make it so,
And my denial would not overthrow
A well-established Deity who lists
Among His attributes that He persists
Through all the evil in the world we know,
Despite the doubt and heresy we show,
Ignoring cynics and the atheists.
And whether you or I have true belief
Is immaterial to One pervasive
Throughout the universe and present through
All space and time and life and death and grief.
So even with the Scriptures not persuasive
We still must live as if this faith is true."

"Now, some will call upon a prophet's name
Without defining what the prophet taught,
The essence of his work an afterthought,
Obscured by holy images and fame.
But if the prophets truly do proclaim
A vision that brings peace to those distraught,
Salvation to the lost, to those who sought
A way to live, should we not do the same?
True, some will seize the easy 'Yes' or 'No',
Too early in their life to understand
What dangers lie ahead, what obstacles,
Not waiting for their minds and souls to grow
Sufficiently to comprehend, withstand,
Or yet, perhaps, accept these principles."

"I have reviewed the work of scientists,
Of Einstein, Newton and Copernicus,
(And some, though worthy, still anonymous),
Empirical and abstract physicists.
I judge their work as honest, it consists
Of careful thought and proof, conspicuous
For working toward a goal, harmonious
Adherence to the rules of realists.
So I believe, and therefore will accept
The first beginning, and the end of time,
And all that comes between, the well-known laws
Of energy and matter that have kept
The balance in the universe, sublime
Stability, implicit without flaws."

"But this reality, however true,
Is not complete, for it cannot explain
Compassion, love, illusion, truth or pain;
These concepts, and the force of life are due
To something more than physics can pursue.
All energy and mass combined abstain
From moral judgments, they do not contain
Those values that the ancient scholars knew.
Then why should I, admitting that creation
Is as it is, and we conform as laws
Of physics dictate, find a way to be
Composed and virtuous without vexation
Within a cold, unyielding world? Because,
There is much value in serenity."

"The fool has said, 'There is no God,' but he
Allows a very narrow definition;
I can agree to share his opposition
To gods with human form and frailty,
And can reject without apology
A God as interventional magician
In crises, or celestial politician,
Exchanging favors for idolatry.
Some others say that God is everywhere,
Ubiquitous throughout the universe,
Somewhat diffuse, and present at a distance,
Uncaring in His isolation there;
But there are none who can deny, or worse,
Condemn a God whose essence is existence."

"Should I consider sacred any place
Within the limits of the universe?
Imagining that *better* or that *worse*
Are qualities applied to things in space?
An echelon of merit cannot grace
A building or a site, nor intersperse
Divine approval with a dreadful curse
Except where human values interface.
The Holy Land is not a land at all,
The sacred places insignificant;
I will ignore where priests and prophets trod
In favor of an unequivocal,
A dedicated higher covenant:
The human spirit is the House of God."

"I will not keep a pagan festival
Nor treat the weekly Sabbath as a day
Apart, distinct and sacred in some way,
For all our hours are holy, integral.
I have no need for any clerical
Authority to live as best I may;
There are no rituals one must obey
Our righteousness is individual.
The Lord our God has told us what to trust
As standards if our lives would rise above
Barbaric levels, thereby to equip
Us with His care: do only what is just,
Exist each minute with a steadfast love,
And walk with God in humble fellowship."

"We never will have proof that God exists,
However, my belief is fundamental,
More practical and sound than transcendental;
As time evades our grasp, still love persists,
Despite agnostics, skeptics, nihilists.
This continuity, not accidental,
(And not inferring some divine parental
Dimension) cannot ever be dismissed.
I know, from personal experience
That love and faith and memory, if pure,
(Despite the strain of time) will all survive,
By having in themselves resilience,
Intrinsic qualities that will endure,
Defying death, and still remain alive."

"Then I will love, and I will not forget,
For love and faith somehow unite us all,
The present and the past, beyond the wall
That separates our consciousness, and yet
The memory endures, and will not let
Our past connections disappear; recall
Of sentiments remembered can enthrall
The senses, and alleviate regret.
Our memory will last as long as breath
Continues, and our consciousness survives;
Remembrance of the past is exquisite.
And faith, the image, reaches past our death,
Creating bridges that prolong our lives;
Yet love is even more, and infinite."

And that was all I thought that I should say,
Although I recognized that moderation,
Along with honor had a part to play,
With charity and moral obligation.
The drama of a life has an array
Of virtues (and of weaknesses); summation
Is hard for simple statements to convey,
And often misses total integration.
But I had done my best to summarize
The principles that govern where I dwell
And bring enlightenment; to my surprise
My mentor only said: "You have done well,
You chose your finest option", whereupon
She smiled in satisfaction, and was gone.

She might have been clairvoyant or omniscient,
But I believe her faith was so sincere
That she could judge what was (or not) sufficient
To create confidence and conquer fear.
And she could see that I had recognized
The varied knowledge, thought and inspiration
I found along my way, and analyzed
Their essences into a new creation.
While traveling the sacred thoroughfare
Combining *kosmos*, human *soul* and *mind*,
I had achieved a sanctuary where
Mortality and life were well-defined.
When all is clarified, then nothing bars
Our view of heaven and of all the stars.

EPILOGUE

SANCTUARY

Now I could see one final figure, waiting
A short way up a gentle, open hill,
And standing by the pathway I must still
Keep on until its end, somehow creating
A closure to the quest, and vindicating
The many years that I had spent until
I reached this place, not able to fulfill
The climax I had been anticipating.
It was a man whom I had seen before,
When early in my journey, in a vision
He told me of his own experience,
When first he stood discouraged on the shore
Of hostile forces, faithlessness, derision,
And questioned whether love had permanence.

And now, he stood before me once again,
The last that I would meet along my way;
And he, most pessimistic of all men,
Had something more that now he wished to say.
For he had followed closely all my course
Through prophets, scientists, philosophers;
Unknown to me, he also knew the source
Responsible when such a thing occurs,
For someone summoned every essence here.
His task was like the others, to express
What he had known of life, no less sincere
Than those whose time on earth was free of stress.
He doubted that a love could stay alive,
Or through a total lifetime could survive.

"Now we have traveled, you and I, until
The ends of both our long and winding roads.
We each have known that loss of love corrodes
The faith that (fragile as a daffodil,
Which fades in harshest sun or hostile chill)
Is sensitive to painful episodes;
Relentless disappointment overloads
Assertive confidence, the strongest will.
But there are many roads that men may travel
And each unique experience will differ,
Some debts and losses merit restitution,
Not all the tangles in a life unravel.
A weak or soft support may well grow stiffer
And some distress may earn its absolution."

"I know that you have kept the faith and gone
Wherever fortune led you, to the end;
Along the way you tried to comprehend
Philosophy, and then you carried on
Through prophets, priests and all the marathon
Of mysteries the universe can send
To anyone, and as a dividend
You studied science for comparison.
By fate, the dreadful dragon called the Sphinx,
Endowed with eagle's wings and lion's claws
Who stands beside the path (or in the middle)
And stares with awful eyes and never blinks,
Did not appear, to illustrate your flaws
Or test your limitations with its riddle."

"The dragon lies in wait and frightens many,
Creating existential apprehension;
Conviction then is shallow, one dimension,
And worthless as the debt of half a penny.
As unendurable as fear and trembling
May be to those affected, to the sick,
There is no panacea that is quick
And those who offer one are just dissembling.
The only true and valid remedy
On which one can rely without illusion
Requires great effort, to achieve a fusion
Of sacred and profound philosophy;
Dynamic love and faith that with each breath
Confirms the seamless flow of life and death."

"Throughout your journey you have heard and seen
The wisest of all men, and they have spoken
Of what they knew or thought, and in between
The chain of understanding stayed unbroken.
Enlightenment is like a fine liqueur
That one receives in small amounts through time,
For if its quality is true and pure
The knowledge it produces is sublime.
As you proceed from youth to adolescence,
And on to adult wisdom, many spent
Great effort to distill the clearest essence;
But more than merely this, they represent
Immortal figures you will not forget,
For we are part of all whom we have met."

He disappeared, and I, again alone,
Could feel that now there was a difference,
For here there was a certain permanence,
An absence of the past that I had known.
Each episode that served as cornerstone
Or reference to orient my sense
Of time was gone, as well as evidence
That I would have a future all my own.
Thus all the past, and everything to come
Was frozen in this present time and place,
As if the world had paused, and undecided,
Had tried to keep its equilibrium
While searching for relief, for breathing space
As all its former energy subsided.

The path that I had followed all these years,
The winding road that seemed so endless then,
Led nowhere now, and even where I 'd been
Had been erased; the signpost disappeared
As in a fog, and nothing volunteered
To serve as any landmark once again;
And I myself was like a denizen
Of some strange landscape having no frontiers.
The space I occupied was vast, unbounded
By any elevation, any hill,
The trees had disappeared as though they never
Existed in the past and once surrounded
My open place; these things no longer fill
A universe now featureless forever.

The sharpness of the contrast of the light
With shadows merges to a softer blend,
That indicates that nature will suspend
The pathway of the sun, which at its height
Showed everything so plainly to our sight.
Our ordinary senses which depend
Upon this source of energy must end,
Reminding us that all things are finite.
The colors also fade, a neutral gray,
At first intense, and then a lesser shade,
Both clouds and earth have smoothed their variation,
And like a monk, assume a dull array;
They drift away like guests who overstayed,
Forgetting limits of their invitation.

The sounds of life that once surrounded me
Were muted now, not only conversation,
But lessons, arguments and disputation;
So many mentors, teaching verbally
Their knowledge of the world, astronomy
And mathematics, God and His creation,
With logic, ethics, life and man's relation
To death and birth, and to eternity.
All these were in the past, now far behind,
There was no more to hear, no more to learn,
But when the sounds had vanished, there was this:
That swirling in the silence of my mind,
In combinations they would still return,
Competing, striving for a synthesis.

REUNION

Now all was finished, there was much to do,
But it was done; the journey had been hard
And long, at times confusing in regard
To things that might be all or partly true.
And there were certain times that I outgrew
An old identity and must discard
A useless shell which only would retard
The period of growth that would ensue.
But I was settled now, in that good place
That I had made, and where there was no fear,
Like bees at night within the honeycomb,
Or astronauts' return from outer space;
So nothing ever could disturb me here,
For I had made my peace, and I was home.

The young man came across the open space,
Illuminated as the evening star
Grows brighter with increasing darkness; far
Away I could not plainly see his face.
For I was old, advancing years erase
The features that were once familiar;
The generations, now dissimilar,
Share fragile memories, once commonplace.
Within these journeys for my education,
The flow of life progressed along its courses,
And with it, I matured and then declined,
My life itself approached its limitation.
But he was still the same, as if the sources
Of death and endless youth were intertwined.

Although he still appeared as he had been,
I sensed a central change internally,
A mental and a moral regimen
Transcending former immaturity.
This shift occurred within the interval
From now back to the time I saw him last,
As if some factors (all reciprocal)
Had changed and compensated for the past.
When mind and body cease, the soul remains;
Into that open space it will expand,
Encompassing the challenge life contains:
To go beyond mere *faith*, to *understand*.
While one may die, another fade away,
The soul will grow, and thus the sum will stay.

The rate of change can vary endlessly;
For some a life is long, allowing growth,
But youth believes in immortality,
Not needing mind or soul, dismissing both.
Then, when a life does not go just as planned
(And God determines when the play will end),
The unaware are wrenched from fairy-land
Into a state they do not comprehend.
Reality, to those who, unprepared,
Have not considered that it might be waiting
Seems harsh and sudden; many have despaired
To feel their hopes and dreams evaporating.
But those with innate moral strength will reach
Into their inner souls to fill the breach.

To those who have been loved, that love remains
Far past their presence or their memory;
For love, if true, is real and it contains
An essence that transcends reality.
If they themselves have loved, it will survive
And be their most enduring legacy;
Relations they have built while still alive
Will serve as beacons, lit eternally.
And so it was with us, for he had been
An ordinary presence in existence
Until his life was interrupted, then
There was a transformation at a distance.
Becoming one with all who lived before,
He found significance, and honor's core.

And I myself had done the best I could,
Along the course I traveled for so long;
If I at stressful times misunderstood
The purpose or the pathway, thought them wrong,
I never doubted that there was some plan,
Some essence that directed where I went
And whom I met, but what Olympian
Could wake such sources of enlightenment?
Whoever summoned teachers such as these:
Profound philosophers of eminence,
The scientists with brilliant theories,
And prophets with exclusive testaments,
That person must have reached a higher plane,
The *Sacred* which transcends the mere *profane*.

I did not know at first what I should say,
Or whether generations could become
United once again so far away
From where they knew an equilibrium.
But from his vantage point he could explain:
"The foolish spend their time in idleness,
Pursuit of pleasure, all of it in vain,
But finally they find it meaningless.
Our life within this world is where we earn
A refuge of a higher category
So neither one of us can now return,
Not you to earth, nor I to purgatory.
Events in life can never be reversed
No matter whether blessed or accursed."

"And though the two of us appear alone
Within an empty, endless universe,
We are a part of all whom we have known;
Whatever is designed will not disperse.
The term of finite, physical existence
Allows a space in which the wise will seek
A way to understand, and bridge the distance
From imperfection to the pure, unique.
Unhappiness in life is separation
From all of history's enlightenment;
To comprehend your place is confirmation
That all your life and time has been well- spent.
This pleasure is no transient abstraction,
But represents eternal satisfaction."

"I loved you, so I drew these streams of thought
Into my hands, and cast them on your way
To guide you, that you might not be distraught
Or wander blindly, somehow go astray.
For ignorance disorients, as night
Eliminates ability to see;
True knowledge gives a welcome second sight,
With understanding comes serenity.
Without assistance, life is never clear,
But filled with complicated mysteries,
Which then create a chronic state of fear
And psychologic insecurities.
So only with a mentor or a guide
Can life as it unfolds be clarified."

The ring was joined, the end and the beginning,
For all was finished, all was now complete;
The force that set the universe to spinning
Had turned upon itself in full retreat.
Replacing passion, ecstasy and wrath,
Serenity and peace now re-enforce
Acceptance of the involuting path,
As love returns forever to its source.
For now the fog of human doubt had fled,
The stars shone brightly through celestial night,
One greater than the rest; in holy dread,
We felt ourselves now turning to the light,
And when the spirit there had blessed us thrice,
We went together into paradise.

End of
"Sacred Verses"

Our fable now is finished.
These our actors were (as I foretold),
All spirits, and are melted in the mist;
And like the filmy fabric of this vision,
The lofty towers, gorgeous palaces,
The solemn temples, this great globe itself,
Yea, all which it inherits shall dissolve,
And like this insubstantial pageant faded,
Leave not a cloud behind.

We are the essence dreams are made of,
And our fleeting lives are rounded with a sleep.

Prospero
"The Tempest"
Wm. Shakespeare